THE CHICAGO SEVEN POLITICAL PROTEST TRIAL

A Headline Court Case

Headline Court Cases

THE CHICAGO SEVEN POLITICAL PROTEST TRIAL

A Headline Court Case

Karen Alonso

Enslow Publishers, Inc.

40 Industrial Road   PO Box 38
Box 398   Aldershot
Berkeley Heights, NJ 07922 Hants GU12 6BP
USA   UK

http://www.enslow.com

Library of Congress Cataloging-in-Publication Data

Alonso, Karen.
  The Chicago Seven political protest trial : a headline court case /
Karen Alonso.
    p. cm. — (Headline court cases)
  Summary: Discusses the trial of Abbie Hoffman, Jerry Rubin, Tom Hayden,
  Rennie Davis, David Dellinger, John Froines, and Lee Weiner for
  activities during the Democratic National Convention of 1968.
  Includes bibliographical references and index.
  ISBN 0-7660-1764-8 (hardcover)
  1. Chicago Seven Trial, Chicago, Ill., 1969-1970—Juvenile literature.
  2. Riots—Illinois—Chicago—History—Juvenile literature. 3. Trials
  (Conspiracy)—Illinois—Chicago—Juvenile literature. [1. Chicago Seven
  Trial, Chicago, Ill., 1969-1970. 2. Trials (Conspiracy)] I. Title. II.
  Series.
KF224.C47 A44 2002
345.73'0243—dc21
                              2002000384

Printed in the United States of America

10 9 8 7 6 5 4 3 2 1

To Our Readers: We have done our best to make sure all Internet addresses in this book
were active and appropriate when we went to press. However, the author and the publisher
have no control over and assume no liability for the material available on those Internet
sites or on other Web sites they may link to. Any comments or suggestions can be sent by
e-mail to comments@enslow.com or to the address on the back cover.

Illustration Credits: All photos are by AP/Worldwide.

Cover Illustrations: AP/Worldwide.

Contents

Introduction

The story of the Chicago Seven takes place in a time of turmoil. Like many other decades in American history, the 1960s brought its own challenges and demands. However, the period from about 1965 through the early 1970s is especially remembered for the level of violence that some demonstrations reached. Much of the conflict during this time occurred between young students and police departments in individual cities.

During the 1960s, many people tried to assert their individuality by the way they dressed. Young men and women wore love beads, headbands, and long flowing clothing. Weaving flowers into their hair, they called themselves "flower children." Many young men wore their hair long and grew beards.

In addition to dressing differently, many people found other ways to express themselves. Many urged peace throughout the world. Some began practicing religions such as Buddhism and Hinduism and other eastern religions, which were uncommon in the United States during the 1960s. Some began using drugs, which they believed would allow them to expand their minds. Some students dropped out of school, believing that formal education was worthless.

A large number of flower children, or hippies, chose to abandon the typical American lifestyle. Some chose to live in a commune, where a large number of people would share the responsibilities and property of the "family." Still others chose not to commit themselves to what they felt was a rigid lifestyle of owning any kind of home at all. These young people simply "lived on the road," wandering from town to town, feeding and clothing themselves and their children as best they could.

A part of the challenge to the usual order in the United States after World War II grew from the collision of many events. In addition to good economic times enjoyed by many Americans during the postwar era, the nation faced the tension of the Cold War. The Cold War was essentially a standoff between the United States and what was then known as the Soviet Union, or USSR, a communist country. Neither nation actually committed acts of war against the other. However, mistrust kept both the United States and the USSR at a constant state of alert, each country waiting for the attack from the other country to begin. At the same time, mutual fear of the catastrophe that could result from war between the two major world powers prevented both countries from beginning actual hostilities.

Americans were alarmed by other events. John F. Kennedy, thirty-fifth president of the United States, was assassinated, as were Malcolm X and Martin Luther King, Jr., leaders of the civil rights movement in the United States.

The assassination of Martin Luther King, Jr., in 1968 led to a tense confrontational atmosphere before the Democratic National Convention the same year. He is pictured here one day before his death.

Another factor was the United States' involvement in the Vietnam War. American soldiers had been sent overseas to fight the communist forces of North Vietnam, which threatened South Vietnam. A large number of Americans, not just young people, were against the war because they felt violence was wrong, regardless of the reason. Still others claimed that American armed forces should not be involved in a conflict that had nothing to do with our own nation's security.

In addition to their basic belief that killing others in war in order to settle a conflict was simply wrong, some Americans were troubled by the alarming number of American soldiers sent to Vietnam. This distress was heightened by reports of the "body count" on the nightly news. The body count was an estimate of soldiers killed, both American and Vietnamese.

Other Americans looked upon communism as a threat that would eventually reach American shores. By sending American troops to Vietnam, they believed, we were helping to crush the spread of communism and give hope to those forced to live in an unjust system. Vice President Hubert H. Humphrey expressed this point of view when he claimed that the antiwar protesters were "incredibly ridiculous" and that they were helping the enemy.[1]

Many young men resented the fact that although they could be sent to Vietnam to fight the North Vietnamese at age eighteen, they were not allowed to vote in a presidential election until they were twenty-one. According to some, the young men of the United States were being sent to fight a war that was being run by older, white men in Congress. These elected officials made the rules for others, but they did not have to fight themselves. These officials, in addition to the usual governmental authorities and large corporations, became known as "the Establishment."

The Establishment was essentially any sort of organization that represented the existing power structure. During the 1960s, the Establishment became the focus of demonstrations that protested the war in Vietnam and other injustices, such as racism. "Radicals" were those who wished to make large and sudden changes in society.

According to one historian, "twenty-two-year-olds set out to change the world."[2] It was the combination of these tensions that produced so much effort to revise everything that many Americans thought of as "normal" in society.

Hippies urged peace throughout the world, but usually dropped out of traditional society, preferring not to protest. Political activists planned demonstrations to urge Americans to demand immediate withdrawal of troops from Vietnam. Unfortunately, these demonstrations often ended in violence. Americans who supported our country's involvement in the war were called "hawks." They, too, expressed their point of view during the demonstrations.

In order to preserve calm, police forces often had to separate the protesters and those who supported the war. At times, even the police were unable to keep order, and the National Guard was called in. A famous photo of this period shows a row of guardsmen pointing rifles at a group of protesters. One protester is strolling along the line of soldiers, sliding the stem of a daisy into the barrel of each gun.

Chaos in the United States

What was the reason for the rebellion in the United States? There was no single reason. However, a number of groups, dissatisfied with the current state of matters in the country, joined in protest that increased in intensity until the commotion in the United States reached its peak.

Women who were active in the women's liberation

movement protested reducing females to mere objects. Scores of American women protested the Miss America Pageant as demeaning. In New York, students at Columbia University took over the school's buildings to protest the university's being used as a tool of the Establishment. Young men fled to Canada rather than obey orders to report for military service and possibly be sent to Vietnam. Robert Kennedy, a potential candidate for the 1968 presidential election and brother to the assassinated President John Kennedy, was himself shot to death moments after a campaign speech.

Demonstrations increased in frequency and hostility, until it seemed that the nightly television news from the mid-1960s into the early 1970s showed one display of anger after another. To a young person at the end of the decade, it seemed as if the world was about to explode from the tension between their generation and the Establishment.

During this time, however, great strides were also made in the civil rights movement. More and more often, African Americans demanded to be given the same rights as white Americans. Protesters objected to unequal treatment in courtrooms and public facilities and to the lack of equal opportunity in competing for jobs. Although Dr. Martin Luther King, Jr., a leader in the peaceful protest movement, urged change through nonviolent means, some demonstrations still became violent.

The 1968 Anti-Riot Act

Congress tried to assist the civil rights leaders by writing laws that would require cities and states to treat all

Americans equally, regardless of race, gender, or religious beliefs. One such proposed law was the Civil Rights Act of 1968. Unfortunately, some lawmakers resisted such laws. Some Southern congressmen in particular feared the aftermath of such a sweeping reform. South Carolina senator Strom Thurmond led a group of lawmakers who blamed the "outside agitators" for the racial demonstrations in the Southern states. The purpose of the Civil Rights Act was to ensure racial equality. However, Thurmond and other senators were apparently concerned that the Civil Rights Act not prompt any of the protests or demonstrations that several states had witnessed in the past. In an effort to pass the Civil Rights Act of 1968, lawmakers agreed on a compromise. The compromise was the addition of a special section to the Civil Rights Act called the 1968 Anti-Riot Act. The Anti-Riot Act stated:

> Whoever travels [between the states] or uses any facility of interstate or foreign commerce, including . . . the mail, . . . telephone, radio, or television, with intent—to incite a riot; or to organize . . . encourage, participate in, or carry on a riot; or to commit any act of violence [which causes a riot to occur]; or to [help] any person [to cause a riot]; shall be fined not more than $10,000, or imprisoned not more than five years, or both."[3]

Still, Americans continued to demonstrate against racial inequality and the war in Vietnam. As the demonstrations grew in frequency, many people, both young and old, found themselves emerging as leaders in the struggle between the generations. The youth found their heroes in popular singers, vocal college students, and poets. Members of the Establishment found their leaders in a more conventional manner. President Lyndon B. Johnson and Chicago's mayor Richard Daley became familiar faces as they responded to charges made by younger Americans.

The tension in the United States in the mid-1960s continued to build until a clash became unavoidable. The expected confrontation occurred in Chicago, Illinois, in summer 1968. In August of that year, the Democratic party

To protesters, Mayor Richard Daley represented "old-time" politics with his tight control of the city of Chicago. He is shown here at the Democratic National Convention.

met in Chicago. Delegates sent from all over the United States came to select their candidate for the next presidential election.

Newspaper and television reporters arrived in Chicago to cover the convention but soon discovered they would record a far more historic event. The clash that would result formed the foundation for the story of the Chicago Seven.

chapter one

TWO FACES OF AMERICA

CHICAGO—During the Democratic National Convention in 1968, the city of Chicago witnessed three days of rioting, demonstrations, and instances of police brutality. Eight people were originally brought to trial for the mass demonstrations. Later, one of the defendants would have his trial separated from the others. The remaining defendants came to be known as the Chicago Seven.

The original eight defendants were protesters from various walks of life. One of the most famous defendants was Abbie Hoffman. At the time of his arrest, Hoffman was thirty years old and one of the founding members of the Youth International Party, or "Yippies." Yippies wanted to encourage a lifestyle that was not weighed down with traditional rules and values. Hoffman became a leader in the radical movement by mixing an aggressive attitude with a sarcastic and biting sense of humor.

Jerry Rubin, another Yippie, was twenty-nine when he was arrested during the Chicago demonstrations. Rubin had an outrageous and theatrical manner of expressing himself, which led to his becoming one of the founders of the Youth International Party.

David Dellinger, fifty-two, was the oldest member of the Chicago Seven. He was also a civil rights advocate and a leader of the National Mobilization to End the War in Vietnam (MOBE). This organization sought peaceful means to bring the Vietnam War to an end. Along with Rennie Davis, a twenty-seven-year-old coordinator for MOBE, Dellinger sought out a strategy to protest the selection of a presidential candidate who would support continuing the United States' involvement in Vietnam.

Tom Hayden, also twenty-seven during the 1968 Democratic National Convention, was a member of the Students for a Democratic Society (SDS). The SDS was a particularly militant group whose stated purpose was to fight against oppression and racism.[1] The group claimed that American universities were terribly corrupted and that they helped the government to wage war by providing research and new weapons. (Twenty years after his trial as a member of the Chicago Seven, Hayden would become part of mainstream politics in California.)

Rennie Davis joined Tom Hayden as codirector of the convention demonstration during its planning stages. Rennie Davis appeared to be a clean-cut young man, but the prosecution would later complain that the defendant was putting on a "little boy next door" act for the jury.[2]

John Froines was a well-educated man, holding degrees

in chemistry from both Berkeley and Yale universities. He also belonged to the Students for a Democratic Society, and he encouraged distribution of scientific information to "scientists of a radical bent."[3] Unlike many of the other defendants in the Chicago Seven trial, Froines dressed simply and did not engage in the more disruptive behavior displayed in court by his fellow defendants.

Lee Weiner, like John Froines, was a part of the academic world. Weiner was working toward a doctoral degree and was a teaching assistant in sociology at Northwestern University.[4] Described later as a "minor figure in the trial," Weiner generally ignored the trial proceedings and read philosophy books as the trial wore on.[5]

Bobby Seale was the only African-American defendant in the Chicago Seven trial. Seale's public recognition came from the fact that he was cofounder of the Black Panther Party, a group that sought equal rights for African Americans. In 1966, Seale formed the Black Panther Party for Self-Defense with Huey Newton. Members of this group claimed that the police officers of Oakland, California, were nothing more than armed invaders of their territory. Protesting police presence in their neighborhoods as a threatening force that harassed African Americans, Black Panthers responded by adopting a semimilitary attitude and organization. Members wore black leather jackets and black berets and openly carried rifles while patrolling the streets of their neighborhood. At that time, carrying an unconcealed weapon was legal in California.

When California state lawmakers tried to pass a law

Bobby Seale (on left) was national chairman of the militant Black Panthers. He is pictured here with fellow activist Huey Newton.

making it illegal to carry unconcealed weapons, thirty members of the Black Panthers carried rifles into the state capitol to protest the bill. One of the founding members of the Black Panthers, Huey Newton, declared that "an unarmed people are either enslaved or subjected to slavery at any given time."[6]

Seale was also a jazz musician and stand-up comedian. He would not be part of the trial for long. He was the eighth defendant, but his trial would be separated from the other seven under bizarre circumstances. The remaining seven defendants then came to be called the Chicago Seven by the press.

The Establishment

Richard J. Daley was mayor of the city of Chicago when the Chicago Seven drama was unfolding. Mayor Daley would later be described as one of the last "old-time political bosses." He was a politician who had a powerful choke-hold on the Chicago Police Department and the Democratic party in the city.[7] Part of Daley's political control had to do with the number of people he had appointed to, or helped to gain, powerful jobs. From the Illinois National Guard to the court system and governor's mansion in Illinois, Daley had contacts, and he exercised his influence liberally. Another factor in Daley's control over the city was his belief in "rigid, inflexible, unquestionable authority." When Daley wanted something to happen in the political arena, "his people" would obey his wishes. Daley was a gruff, heavy-handed mayor, who had vowed during this period of protests that rioters and looters would be shot on sight.[8]

Celebration of Life

In December 1967, Abbie Hoffman and Jerry Rubin began planning their strategy to protest the 1968 Democratic Convention in Chicago. At the convention, the Democratic party would choose its candidate to run in the upcoming presidential election. Abbie Hoffman and the Yippies saw the convention as a "convention of death."[9] Under the then-current president, Lyndon B. Johnson, the United States had become more involved in the Vietnam War. Tom Hayden and Rennie Davis were members of the Students for a Democratic Society. The group strongly opposed U.S. involvement in the Vietnam War. Hayden and Davis met with Abbie Hoffman and Jerry Rubin to plan the Festival of Life. The festival was meant to stand in stark contrast to the more serious Democratic National Convention.

The Yippies' intent was to mock the typical middle-class American values. For its part, SDS hoped to call attention to the number of lives lost in Vietnam. Whatever the background of the individual protesters, each wanted to protest effectively against the war, racism, and the "unresponsiveness of the Democratic Party."[10]

Abbie Hoffman planned to disrupt the legitimate convention with "monkey-warfare highjinks."[11] Partly as a practical joke, partly as a statement, Hoffman announced plans to nominate a pig to run for the president of the United States. (At the time, some American youth referred to police officers and other people in authority as "pigs.") Hoffman even proposed painting cars to look like Chicago taxis, picking up delegates to the convention, and dropping them off somewhere outside Illinois. However, Hoffman claimed that their strategy never included plans for "organized violence."[12]

The plans for the Festival of Life included camping out in Chicago's city parks for those young people who planned to attend. Attendees would be welcome to join lessons in karate, self-defense, and "snake dancing." A snake dance is a paradelike dance in which the participants move with their arms linked together. The object was to snake dance through the streets to offer some bodily protection to the demonstrators.[13] Protesters moved through the streets in this tight-knit formation in order to keep police officers from easily moving through the mass of protesters. Although this offered poor protection to anyone but those snake dancers in the very center of the group, the young protesters made the most of what they had. Earlier demonstrations throughout the country had brought police action, and the festival planners wished to provide protest marchers with the means to protect themselves.

In order to allow a large number of people to join in the Festival of Life, the organizers wanted participants to be able to camp out in Chicago's Lincoln Park. Convention delegates usually book hotel rooms far in advance. However, the young protesters either could not afford to pay for a hotel room or rejected the more conventional comforts of a hotel.

To meet the demands for the large numbers expected,

Hoffman applied for the necessary permit to camp out in the park. He believed that, if the permit were granted, then one hundred thousand people would attend the festival, ensuring only peaceful demonstrations. If the permit were denied, then the campers would be guilty of illegal trespassing. "The numbers would be fewer, but they would be angrier," Hoffman said.[14]

David Stahl, chief negotiator for the city of Chicago, denied permits for camping in the park and for any organized demonstrations. Chicago mayor Richard Daley supported Stahl's refusal to grant permits. The protesters hoped that the permits would be granted at the last minute, since city officials were evasive during negotiation sessions.[15]

Matters were made worse when communication broke down between city officials and the protesters. Conflict and suspicion between the two groups led to the spread of outrageous stories. Rumors spread among the protesters that city sewers were being prepared for jails and that police dogs were being trained to attack demonstrators.[16]

As a result of these rumors, several SDS chapters, rock stars, and *Rolling Stone* magazine cautioned young people to avoid the demonstration in Chicago. Martin Luther King, Jr., and presidential candidate Bobby Kennedy had recently been assassinated. Protesters feared that some of them might also be killed during the demonstration.

For their part, city officials feared that the demonstrations would become destructive. Possibly arising from Abbie Hoffman's announced highjinks, rumors spread at City Hall that demonstrators would try to kill Democratic candidates and that the city's water supply would be poisoned with harmful drugs. In response to these rumors, city officials ran barbed-wire fences around the amphitheater where the convention was to take place. Additionally, all Chicago police officers were placed on twelve-hour shifts to meet any violence.

Mistrust and fear were planted on both sides. It seemed that a violent confrontation between Chicago's city police and the youthful protesters was becoming inevitable. Either side could have prevented the episode that would unfold in Chicago's parks during the summer of 1968. However, protesters and the Establishment both marched forward toward what would become the historic days of the 1968 Democratic National Convention.

chapter two

THE CONVENTION

THE MAYOR AND THE PROTESTERS—Mayor Richard Daley represented almost everything the young protesters disliked about the Establishment. He was in a position of authority and exerted his power forcefully. Daley had already dealt with the violent aftermath of Dr. Martin Luther King's assassination by ordering the police department to be tough on looters and rioters. The police had been ordered to "shoot to kill" anyone who threatened the city's peace.[1]

Those who came to Chicago to demonstrate against the Democratic nomination of Hubert Humphrey were equally committed to making their plans clear. Whether the protesters were hippies, Yippies, pacifists, or the clean-cut supporters of Senator Eugene McCarthy, they wanted to be sure that the world knew of their dissatisfaction with the then-present state of the world. McCarthy was the candidate preferred by many young Americans who were

Many protesters at the Democratic National Convention supported Senator Eugene McCarthy for president because of his opposition to American involvement in Vietnam.

becoming involved in politics in 1968. This support stemmed largely from the fact that Senator McCarthy opposed American involvement in Vietnam. He also won support from those who believed that politics in the United States was "fixed," or the outcome predetermined, since McCarthy wanted to change the way American politics worked. He favored open discussions and debate of issues during the Chicago convention.

Although Eugene McCarthy welcomed active involvement from young Americans, he opposed asking his young followers to follow him to Chicago during convention week. Although this would have swelled the number of demonstrators who arrived for the Festival of Life, McCarthy feared that he would be responsible for any injuries suffered by demonstrators who were sure to be caught up in some confrontation with authorities.

Months before the convention, the radicals advertised their promise to "turn the city upside down."[2]

Curfews and Karate

In an attempt to preserve order and prevent protesters from sleeping in the park, Chicago officials called for an 11:00 P.M. curfew. The curfew required that all visitors leave the park by the specified time or risk being arrested. Many of the protesters who planned to sleep in the park refused to change their plans. They believed that city officials would eventually change their minds about the curfew or at least look the other way when curfew came.[3] Some found other sleeping arrangements, claiming that sleeping in the park past curfew was not as important as "living our revolution there the rest of the day."[4]

In addition to practicing snake dancing, Yippies offered lessons on karate, judo, and using a rolled-up magazine in order to protect themselves from attack. In spite of all the planning, the various groups of protesters suffered setbacks just before the Festival of Life was to begin. A seminary near Lincoln Park refused the Yippies the use of their parks for sleeping. Then, several rock groups that were to perform for the protesters on Sunday, August 25, 1968, canceled their appearances.

In spite of these setbacks and the threat of possible violence, the festival was to go on. Just before the convention began, one newspaper writer predicted that a violent clash between demonstrators and police was unavoidable. According to Richard Strout, the news media was to blame in large part for the anticipated violence:

> The mildest parade of young people brings a TV camera crew like a hook-and-ladder truck to a three-alarm fire. Any youngster who will denounce the authorities finds himself surrounded by a ring of . . . microphones. The press has talked so much about violence that . . . it will look silly if it doesn't get it.[5]

In fact, the American public had every reason to expect violent confrontation. During the convention, protesters distributed a pamphlet that reflected the dissenters' attitude toward customary life in the United States. The pamphlet urged the reader:

National Guardsmen face hippies and antiwar protesters on the street in front of Chicago's Hilton Hotel on August 28, 1968.

Disobey your parents. . . . Burn your money. Break down the family, church, nature, city, economy, turn life into an art form and theatre of the soul. What is needed is a generation of people who are . . . crazy . . . angry . . . childish and mad.[6]

The Explosion

The 1968 Democratic National Convention was scheduled for the week of August 25, 1968. As promised, the Festival of Life was in full swing. Approximately five thousand people were listening to the band MC5, handing out flowers, and listening to poetry. However, the joyful celebration planned by the Yippies appeared to have been affected by the anticipated confrontation with the police.

One witness to the scene said that the protesters "didn't have any plan. It was supposed to have been a festival of life, but I didn't see any happy people. Everybody I walked past looked depressed and aimless . . . But when it got dark, then things started to speed up."[7]

At 10:30 P.M., Chicago police circulated through the park with bullhorns, announcing the closing of the park for the 11:00 o'clock curfew. Police officers told the crowd that the park was closing.[8] Abbie Hoffman urged the young people to stay in the park.

Just after the 11:00 P.M. curfew, the police charged into the park, releasing tear gas and swinging their nightsticks at the demonstrators. Abbie Hoffman described the scene:

> Our determination to stay in the park became as firm as the city's to drive us into the streets. During the next two nights . . . barricades were erected. Tear gas clouds drifted from the park, as did the mass of demonstrators chased by police cars and flying wedges of cops. Like enraged bulls taunted by red flags, the men in blue charged in all directions.[9]

Although most of the protesters were peaceful and listening to the band, several were antagonizing the police, shouting obscenities. One young person flicked a lighted cigarette at a police officer, and several others threw rocks. Still other protesters "ran around smashing car windows and vandalizing buildings."[10]

The worst of the protests would continue through Wednesday, August 28, 1968.

With each confrontation between police and protesters, many arrests were made. During the four days of violence

A protester confronts National Guard troops in front of the Chicago Hilton Hotel.

and protest, the eight original defendants in the Chicago Seven trial were arrested.

Tom Hayden was arrested on Monday, after a police officer saw him letting the air out of a police car tire. Rennie Davis would be arrested shortly afterward. According to an undercover police officer, Davis urged the protesters to further violence. Using a megaphone, Rennie Davis reportedly shouted at people to "fight the pigs."[11]

Davis maintains that his purpose was always to keep the demonstration a nonviolent event. His version of the events surrounding his arrest was that, at a moment when the crowd of demonstrators and police were about to explode into a riot, he informed police through a bullhorn that his crowd had been "secured . . . and if they would just pull back and withdraw, then we could continue with our rally."[12] However, the police went forward, and according to Davis, about fifty policemen were shouting "Kill Davis!"[13] Davis said, "The first hit was to the head, and drove me to the ground; and then it was just being beaten on the back over and over again."[14]

On Wednesday morning, Abbie Hoffman was arrested while having breakfast. Hoffman claimed he did not want to be photographed that day, so he wrote an obscene word on his forehead with lipstick to discourage photographers. According to Hoffman, police dragged him "right across the table, through the bacon and eggs, across the floor . . . and . . . into a waiting paddy wagon."[15]

Later that same day, some protesters attempted to lower the American flag opposite the Conrad Hilton Hotel, the convention's headquarters. When the police moved in to take the flag, Jerry Rubin urged demonstrators to attack the police.[16]

In nearby Grant Park, Bobby Seale, David Dellinger, and Tom Hayden addressed a crowd of about ten thousand people. Informants reported that Tom Hayden told the audience to meet violence with violence: "Make sure that if blood is going to flow, let it flow all over the city!"[17] At the same gathering, Bobby Seale, leader of the Black Panthers, reminded the crowd of the history of racism and oppression in the United States.

Seale was a last-minute replacement speaker and had not even met the other seven defendants until shortly before the trial. He was arrested because he urged demonstrators to fight. "Pick up a gun. And pull that spike out from the wall. Because if you pull it on out and if you shoot well, all I'm gonna do is pat you on the back."[18]

At another section of the park, undercover police officer Irwin Bock met with Lee Weiner and John Froines. According to the police officer, Froines stated that the demonstrators needed more ammunition to use against the police. Weiner responded by suggesting Molotov cocktails (homemade fire bombs) be used against a chosen target somewhere in Chicago.

When the worst of the rioting, demonstrations, and police attacks had finally calmed down, many young men and women had been arrested for their various activities. However, eight men would be selected to stand trial for the rioting and destruction that had taken place in Chicago.

Rennie Davis would later comment that "in choosing the eight of us, the government has lumped together all the strands of dissent in the sixties."[19]

United States attorney general Ramsey Clark felt that the events in the city that summer had been a "police riot."[20] Therefore, he was intent on prosecuting eight Chicago police officers who had been charged with brutality against demonstrators. Mayor Daley was outraged by the bad image this would give to his city and the men and women of the police whose job was to protect that city's residents. The Illinois attorney general decided to prosecute the same number of demonstrators.[21] In the end, it was the trial of the demonstrators that captured the nation's attention.

chapter three

THE TRIAL

INDICTMENTS—A defendant cannot simply be brought directly from the police station to the courtroom to stand trial. Under the United States' system of justice, a grand jury is appointed to review the charges and evidence against a potential defendant. The grand jury does not decide the guilt or innocence of a particular defendant. Rather, it decides whether there is enough evidence to require that the defendant stand trial. If it finds that there is enough evidence, the grand jury issues an indictment, or formal charge of a crime.

On March 20, 1969, a grand jury issued indictments against David Dellinger, Rennie Davis, Thomas Hayden, Abbie Hoffman, Jerry Rubin, Lee Weiner, John Froines, and Bobby Seale. According to the words of the indictments, these men had conspired, or secretly agreed, to travel among several states with the intent to encourage and participate in a riot. The eight men had also participated in riots or acted in such a way as to cause a riot.[1]

The indictments also charged that John Froines and Lee Weiner taught others to make a bomb to damage the underground parking garage at Grant Park. Later, the defendants were arraigned, or informed of the charges against them. The eight men came from vastly different backgrounds; in fact, they had not all even met each other until they were arraigned. Abbie Hoffman would remark that the charge of conspiracy was ridiculous. According to Hoffman, the eight supposed conspirators could not even "agree on lunch."[2]

The Chicago Seven defendants share a light moment at a news conference during their trial. They are from left, standing: Abbie Hoffman, John Froines, Lee Weiner, Dave Dellinger, Rennie Davis, and Tom Hayden. Seated in front are Jerry Rubin and his girlfriend, Nancy Kurshan.

Nonetheless, the Chicago conspiracy trial was about to begin.

Inside the Courtroom

The eight men charged appeared for their trial on September 24, 1969, in the United States District Court for the Northern District of Illinois, Eastern Division.[3] Judge Julius Hoffman presided over the trial. Although he shared a common name with one of the defendants, Judge Hoffman was not related to Abbie Hoffman.

At the age of seventy-four when the trial began, Judge Hoffman was as different from the defendants as he could possibly be. Hoffman was a formal man who followed courtroom rules strictly. He was short and balding, and the defendants referred to him among themselves as Mr. Magoo (a cartoon character).[4] Chicago attorneys who were familiar with Judge Hoffman's style claimed that Hoffman always saw the "defense in any criminal case as the enemy and his duty to help put them away."[5]

Two men were chosen to prosecute the eight defendants. As prosecutors, Thomas Foran and Richard Schultz would present the government's arguments to the jury, hoping to prove that the eight defendants were guilty of violating the Civil Rights Act of 1968.

William Kunstler and Leonard Weinglass represented the eight defendants. Like their clients, Kunstler and Weinglass displayed little respect for the judge and courtroom manners.[6] William Kunstler would go on to become one of the United States' most famous lawyers,

Police remove a demonstrator from Chicago's Grant Park during the convention.

often representing clients who were very unpopular. To some observers, it seemed that the trial would be a reflection of the differences between generations that had erupted during convention week in Chicago.[7]

Selecting the Jury

Each trial begins with selection of a jury. During the selection process, both prosecution and defense attorneys are allowed to ask potential jurors questions in order to determine whether an individual might be prejudiced for or against one side. If so, that person can be excused from jury service.

William Kunstler and Leonard Weinglass requested that Judge Hoffman ask jurors a number of questions about their attitudes on lifestyle. The proposed questions included, "Do you have any hostile feelings toward persons whose lifestyles differ from your own?"[8] They also wanted to ask the jurors whether they would let their son or daughter "marry a Yippie."[9] However, Judge Hoffman did not ask prospective jurors all the questions proposed by the defense.

When the twelve jurors were finally selected, the panel included ten women and two men. The defense attorneys felt that four of the jurors might be sympathetic to the defendants' case.[10] Those four included two African-American women, a young woman wearing a miniskirt, and a fourth woman who came to court carrying a book written by an African-American writer.[11]

The Uproar

Even before the first witness was called, the basic impatience and disregard that the people on one side of the issue had for those on the other side made itself clear. Mr. Schultz began his opening remarks to the jury. Opening remarks consist of a summary of the issues that the attorney for each side wishes to prove during the trial.

As Richard Schultz was identifying each of the defendants, Tom Hayden stood and raised his clenched fist in the then-popular "Power to the people" sign. Judge Hoffman immediately sent the jury from the room and warned Mr. Hayden not to repeat "the fist shaking."[12]

When Abbie Hoffman was pointed out to the jurors, he stood and blew a kiss to the jury. Judge Hoffman immediately told the jury not to pay attention to the kiss "thrown by defendant Hoffman and the defendant is directed not to do that sort of thing again."[13]

Mr. Weinglass made his opening remarks to the jury on behalf of the defense. When his comments were complete, Judge Hoffman asked whether there were any other lawyers who wanted to make an opening statement to the jury. At that time, Bobby Seale, who had been silent until that point, rose and walked toward the lectern with a yellow legal pad in his hand.

Judge Hoffman had assumed that Kunstler and Weinglass represented Mr. Seale. However, Bobby Seale would allow no other lawyer than Charles R. Garry to represent him. Unfortunately, Garry was unavailable because of recent surgery. Hoffman stated that Kunstler could make another opening statement on Mr. Seale's behalf.

This was not acceptable to either Kunstler or Seale, as a defendant in a criminal case has the right to be represented by his or her counsel of choice. Nevertheless, Judge Hoffman ordered that the trial continue. That decision ignited one of the most disgraceful episodes in an American courtroom. However, the real explosion would not come until the trial was actually under way.

chapter four

THE PROSECUTION'S CASE

THE COURTROOM—The prosecution's task was to show that the eight defendants had secretly agreed to encourage others to riot during the 1968 Chicago convention. They also planned to show that the defendants meant to provoke the Chicago police and the National Guard into violence, making it seem that the police started the violence in the first place.

Another part of the government's theory of the facts was that the Festival of Life, announced by the Yippies as a peaceful celebration of life, was intended only to lure large numbers of demonstrators to Chicago. Once there, the crowds could be incited, encouraged by the festival organizers, to riot.

The prosecution also theorized that the "volunteer marshals" were not meant to patrol and control the crowd, but to lead the crowds in aggressive moves and rioting. The government also intended to show that the defendants wished to create a public display of violence on the night that the Democratic candidate for the presidency was announced. On that night, the defendants knew that the "world would be watching," so that their message would reach the greatest number of people.[1]

However, before the prosecution had questioned the first of its witnesses, William Kunstler began court proceedings on the morning of September 30, 1969, with a motion to disqualify the judge. During Mr. Weinglass's opening statements on behalf of the defendants, Judge Hoffman had ruled that the defense attorney constantly ignored the direction of the Court and that his conduct was insulting and arrogant. Mr. Kunstler then pointed out that he had a witness who would testify to hearing the judge refer to the other defense attorney out of court as that "wild man Weinglass."

According to Kunstler, these statements proved that Judge Hoffman was partial to the prosecution and that his unfair attitude would prejudice the jury against the defendants. Judge Hoffman simply denied the motion, saying that the defense's motion did not "state grounds for the relief sought."[2] Hoffman would not comment about the statements he supposedly made about the defense or its attorneys.

Prosecution Witnesses

Prosecutor Thomas Foran called David Stahl to the witness stand. As Chicago's administrative officer, Stahl managed the budget and operations of the city. The prosecutor called Stahl to the stand to testify about certain statements made by Jerry Rubin while negotiating for permits for the demonstrations.

Prosecutor Thomas Foran ran for the office of governor of Illinois after the Chicago Seven trial, but he was not elected.

David Stahl stated that during the negotiations, Rubin announced that there would be classes in self-defense, since Chicago had a "national reputation of being a hostile system."[3] He also related Abbie Hoffman's promise to "tear up the town and the Convention" and his statement about being "willing to die in Lincoln Park."[4] This testimony was meant to show that the defendants desired a show of violence in Chicago for the entire world to witness.

The prosecution also attempted to suggest that the Festival of Life was planned by Hoffman to get money from the city of Chicago rather than to exercise free speech, as the defendant claimed. To that end, David Stahl related Hoffman's statement that if the city of Chicago were smart, it would "give him a hundred thousand dollars and he would leave town."[5]

Next, Schultz called Robert Murray to the stand. Murray had been a plainclothes police officer during the 1968 demonstrations. He testified about statements made by defendant Jerry Rubin. According to the Chicago police sergeant, he watched Jerry Rubin talking to an ABC news reporter.

During the conversation, the news reporter announced that he and the crew were leaving for coffee. At that point, Murray stated, Rubin had said, "Wait, don't go right now. We're going out in the ball field," and "we want to see what these pigs are going to do about it."[6] When the news crew agreed to wait, Jerry Rubin began shouting to a crowd of demonstrators, "waving his arms," and "shouting obsceni- ties," according to Murray.[7]

Robert Murray also stated that Rubin led a group of protesters over to a group of about ten police officers. At the same time, Rubin was shouting that the park belonged to the people.[8] According to Murray, the police officers were backed up against a wall, with Rubin and the others hurling insults and obscene statements at the police officers.

Finally, Rubin shouted, "Look at them. They look so tough with their arms folded. Take off your guns, and we'll fight you hand to hand."[9] Murray stated that the crowd began to "yell the same things." When Rubin flicked a cigarette butt at the officers, the crowd followed by throwing "cans, bottles, stones . . . paper . . . [and] food wrappings."[10]

According to Murray, the episode lasted for ten minutes. While the crowd of two hundred people continued to scream at the ten officers, Robert Murray said, he observed Rubin walking backward out of the crowd. The prosecution presented this testimony to show that the defendants intended to provoke violence from the police. This testimony also suggested that the leaders

Judge Julius J. Hoffman presided over the controversial Chicago Seven trial.

and volunteer marshals were not meant to control the crowd but to lead them in aggressive action.

Mysterious Letters

The prosecution did not proceed far in its presentation of evidence. The morning session on the first day of trial would set a pattern that would last throughout the entire proceedings. Questioning witnesses would have to wait, as Foran requested a meeting in the judge's private chambers. Attorneys for both sides followed the judge to his office, where Foran revealed that two jurors had received mysterious letters the night before. One of the jurors was the young miniskirted woman, Kristi King, whom the defense felt was open to their side.

The letters were written with a felt-tip pen and stated simply, "We are watching you." The letters were signed, "The Black Panthers."[11] Could the letters be taken at face value, as the prosecution suggested? If so, Miss King might possibly feel threatened by those sympathetic to the defense and should be removed from the jury.

On the other hand, the defendants claimed that the Federal Bureau of Investigation (FBI) had probably written the letters, in order to set up for dismissal those jurors who were sympathetic to the eight defendants. Bobby Seale expressed this point of view in a message to reporters. He accused the FBI of sending the letters as "part of a low-life racist attack . . . to tamper with the jury and make the Panthers look bad."[12] The other seven defendants argued that

Chairman Fred Hampton of the Illinois Black Panther party speaks with the press during a protest outside the courthouse during the Chicago Seven trial. Looking on is Dr. Benjamin Spock, a pediatrician, popular author, and peace activist.

threatening the jury would hardly be a sensible way to make their case.

While those remaining in the courtroom waited for the return of the judge and attorneys, Rennie Davis passed donuts and jellybeans around the courtroom. When court was back in session later that afternoon, Judge Hoffman solved the problem of the threatened juror by removing Kristi King from the panel. Kay Richards replaced her. Like King, Richards was twenty-three years old.

Judge Hoffman then ordered that the jury be sequestered, or confined away from others, for the rest of the trial. A jury is sequestered when there is a danger that outsiders may try to bribe or threaten the jury members in order to influence their verdict, or decision. For the next five months, the Chicago jury would stay at a hotel only three blocks from the courthouse.

To courtroom observers, it seemed that all troubling matters had finally been resolved, and the real trial should now begin. However, it would soon be obvious that the drama surrounding the Chicago trial had only just begun.

chapter five

BOBBY SEALE OBJECTS

HELD IN CONTEMPT—The trial of the eight Chicago defendants had already become what many would call a "circus." The defendants made constant interruptions, and Judge Hoffman responded by making an equal number of contempt charges against all eight of the defendants. A defendant shows contempt for the court when he or she deliberately does anything that is meant to defy the court's dignity or authority or delay the administration of justice. By constantly interrupting Judge Hoffman, who was the administrator of the court and its proceedings, the defendants were showing contempt of court. A contempt of court charge is very serious. A defendant or lawyer found in contempt of court can be fined or even be sent to jail for the offense. Judge Hoffman had the power to punish the eight defendants for their acts of contempt, but he would not do so until the end of the trial.

Even the defense attorneys were frustrated with

Judge Hoffman's refusal to allow Bobby Seale to question witnesses. Under the Sixth Amendment to the United States Constitution, a defendant in a criminal case has the right to counsel of his choice. Seale expected that William Kunstler would represent him only for requests made to the court before the trial began. He had selected Charles R. Garry to represent him during his trial in Chicago. However, Garry was recovering from a serious illness and could not appear on Seale's behalf.

Another complication existed regarding Seale's representation for the Chicago trial. Unlike the other seven defendants who were free to leave the courthouse at the end of each day, Bobby Seale was brought to jail when the daily court proceedings were concluded. Seale was kept in custody because he faced more serious charges in Connecticut. Once the Chicago trial ended, he would be required to stand trial again in Connecticut for murder. So, in essence, he was being held in jail on the murder charges.

Therefore, on October 20, 1969, Bobby Seale asked Judge Hoffman if he could file a motion, or request, with the court. The judge granted Seale's request. Bobby Seale stated that since he could not have the counsel of his choice, he should be allowed to act as own counsel.

In order to perform that task effectively, the defendant requested his release from jail. The necessary tasks Seale mentioned included cross-examining witnesses and calling witnesses of his own choice. He also requested the right to make all motions to the court and defend those motions in his own defense. When Seale finished his request, Kunstler rose to tell the judge that the other seven defendants supported Seale.

The prosecution argued that Seale was simply attempting to disrupt the trial. After all, he was already represented by counsel—Kunstler and Weinglass. The judge agreed with the prosecution, noting that at the beginning of the trial, William Kunstler had stated that he would represent four of the defendants and Weinglass would represent the other four. He added that a judge need not grant a motion for a defendant to represent himself when it might disrupt the proceedings or delay or confuse the trial.[1]

Judge Hoffman's decision to refuse Bobby Seale's request touched off the most explosive episodes of the conspiracy trial. Seale constantly demanded to be allowed to cross-examine prosecution witnesses who testified about his participation during the demonstrations. Judge Hoffman responded to each request by reminding the defendant that he was not allowed to speak in court unless he was testifying. He was already represented by counsel who could question witnesses on his behalf.

At one point, Seale refused to obey the judge's orders to be seated, and his request to question a witness was again denied. Bobby Seale answered the judge:

> Every other word you say is denied, denied, denied . . . and you begin to oink in the faces . . . of the people of this country. That is what you begin to represent, the corruptness of this rotten government. . . .[2]

Each exchange between judge and defendant became more heated until the conflict erupted during the testimony of William Frapolly, a college student who was also an undercover Chicago police officer during the summer of 1968. On October 28, 1969, Judge Hoffman denied Bobby Seale's request to cross-examine Mr. Frapolly.

The conflict between defendant and judge was now direct and personal. Seale restated his position that he was his own counsel. Hoffman responded that Seale was "not doing very well" for himself.[3] Seale answered: "Yes, that's because you violated my constitutional rights, Judge Hoffman. That's because you violated them overtly, deliberately, in a very racist manner."[4]

The judge responded to Seale's remarks by reminding the defendant of the power of the court. Hoffman told Mr. Seale that "the court has the right to gag you. I don't want to do that. Under the law you may be gagged and chained to your chair."[5]

Finally, Judge Hoffman lost patience and called a recess until the following morning. All eight defendants refused to rise to show respect for the judge as he prepared to exit the room. This refusal could easily be interpreted by the judge as another act of contempt of court.

The following day, October 29, 1969, Judge Hoffman addressed each of the defendants' refusal to rise on the previous afternoon. With the jury excused for the day, Hoffman told Kunstler that over the noon hour, he would "reflect on whether they are good risks for bail and I shall give serious consideration to the termination of their bail if you can't control your clients."[6] The judge was threatening to make the defendants stay in jail when they were not in the courtroom.

Defendant Bobby Seale's demand to represent himself was rejected by Judge Hoffman. Seale is pictured here (on the left) with Jesse Jackson in a 1972 photo.

On behalf of his clients, William Kunstler answered that the other seven defendants supported Seale's right to defend himself, and that if "that is the price of their bail then I guess that will have to be the price of their bail."[7]

Attorney Kunstler also related his clients' feelings that Judge Hoffman had violated their constitutional rights in many ways. Kunstler outlined them for the court:

- Hoffman had ordered the arrest of four attorneys who had been hired only to assist in making pretrial motions to the court. According to Judge Hoffman, they were in contempt of court because they failed to appear in court when the trial started. The jury might be prejudiced against his clients because of this.

- According to Kunstler, there had been a "constant rain" of threats of contempt charges from Hoffman against clients and their attorneys, and this was prejudicial to his clients.

- Hoffman was an intimidating presence over the proceedings from the very beginning. This was supposedly an attempt to discourage defense attorneys from making a vigorous defense to charges against them.

- Hoffman allowed an "armed camp atmosphere" in the courtroom. Nineteen marshals crowded the aisles of the courtroom. Kunstler argued that the jury would be certain to be prejudiced by this, with the result that the defendants would be denied a fair trial.[8]

Foran responded by pointing out that both Bobby Seale and William Kunstler had made more than enough objections to Judge Hoffman's insistence that Kunstler would represent Seale. Therefore, if the issue over whether or not Bobby Seale could represent himself during the trial was enough to gain Seale an appeal, there was already more than enough evidence on the record. According to Foran, constant interruption of the trial on that point could only be for the purpose of disrupting the trial.[9]

Foran also stated that the United States government was the only one in the world that provided for the "opportunity to change the law by law and not by disruptive tactics and not by the grossest kind of attack on the very values of the law itself."[10]

With Foran and Kunstler having finished their arguments, Bobby Seale tried once more to argue his point of view. When Judge Hoffman refused, Seale pressed the issue, reminding the court that he had a right to defend himself in the courtroom: "[The] law protects my right not to be discriminated against in my legal defense. Why don't you recognize that? It's a form of racism, racism is what stopped my argument."[11]

Judge Hoffman could tolerate no more interruption from defendant Bobby Seale. He ordered the marshal to take "that defendant into the room in there and deal with him as he should be dealt with. . . ."[12]

The marshals took Seale to a nearby room, handcuffed him to a metal chair, and silenced him by tying a gag over his mouth. When he was brought back to the courtroom in this condition, Seale tried to continue to argue about his civil rights. Hoffman told the marshals that the gag was not working well enough and ordered another recess so that the gag could be made tighter.

Throughout this bizarre exchange, none of the other seven defendants rose to show respect for the judge. One of the female jurors wept as she saw Seale struggle against the gag and straps.

Rennie Davis rose when the jury returned and told them that Seale "was being tortured while you were out of this room by these marshals. They come and torture him while you are out of the room. It is terrible what is happening."[13]

Kunstler complained to the judge that his methods were a disgrace. He asked the judge if he was "going to stop this medieval torture that is going on in this courtroom? . . . This is no longer a court of order."[14] Had the courtroom gone completely out of control? To Abbie Hoffman, one of the defendants, the trial was a "circus."[15]

Finally, even Judge Hoffman could see that there was little point in continuing the trial with Bobby Seale as one of the defendants. Hoffman declared that Seale was guilty on all of the charges of contempt of court throughout the trial to that point. The judge imposed a sentence of three months in prison for each of the acts of contempt, and he declared that the individual sentences should run one after the other. Bobby Seale had such a large number of contempt charges against him that his jail sentence would amount to four years in prison.

With the sentence imposed, Judge Hoffman declared the trial of Bobby Seale a mistrial. A mistrial is one that ends before its usual conclusion, because of some extraordinary event, such as the death of a juror or because the jury cannot agree on a verdict. Although Hoffman did not state specifically the reason for declaring a mistrial, the ongoing dispute between judge and defendant about his right to defend himself in court was certainly enough to require that a new and separate trial be held for Seale.

The marshals removed Bobby Seale from the courtroom. He left still arguing that Judge Hoffman could not "call it a mistrial. I'm put in jail for four years for nothing?"[16]

Bobby Seale would receive another trial. The remaining seven defendants were required to continue their trial under the authority of Judge Hoffman. However, the rest of their trial would be no less chaotic.

Finally, it was the defense's turn to present its own theory of the facts. The Chicago Seven would prove to be as unconventional in the presentation of their defense as they had been during the presentation of the government's case against them. The next chapter describes the unique events and defense presented by the Chicago Seven's attorneys, William Kunstler and Leonard Weinglass.

chapter six

THE DEFENSE

DEFENSE LAWYERS— When William Kunstler arrived in Chicago for the trial of the Chicago Seven in 1969, he had already gained quite a reputation as a defender of those arrested for protesting the war in Vietnam.[1] Since he chose to represent such controversial clients, William Kunstler drew a great deal of attention from the American public. Described by some as a fearless defender of civil rights, Kunstler was despised by others as an arrogant man seeking attention from the media.[2]

The other attorney appearing on behalf of the Chicago Seven was Leonard Weinglass. Although he was less colorful a figure than Kunstler, Weinglass enjoyed the reputation of being the better prepared of the two, often working long hours into the night to get ready for trial.

Once the government finished presenting its case against the seven defendants, William Kunstler made a motion asking the court to acquit all seven defendants. According to the defense attorney, the prosecutors had failed to prove their case of conspiracy against the Chicago Seven.

First, Kunstler argued that all the acts complained of by the government had been performed by the defendants within the city of Chicago. The defense attorney pointed out that the statute, or law, plainly required that there must be travel from one state to another in order for the federal law to apply to these defendants.

William Kunstler also pointed out that there was no conspiracy, or secret meetings among the defendants. According to Kunstler, all the meetings in preparation for the demonstration were open and held in places where "anyone could walk in, and anyone did . . . from informers to people who were training as marshals, to the press."[3]

On behalf of the government, Mr. Schultz was quick to point out that each of the defendants did travel from one state to another. "We have them out of the state, then we have them here . . . and when they got here they did specific acts in the street or in the park of inciting a crowd to violence, to riot."[4]

Judge Hoffman responded that he would look at the arguments in the best possible light on behalf of the government, so that the trial could continue. Therefore, the defense motion to acquit the Chicago Seven was denied.

The Defense Calls Witnesses

The defense team approached the same set of facts but tried to show that the reason for the protesters' behavior was not to encourage others to riot during convention week in

Chicago, but rather to exercise their civil right to protest the war in Vietnam and the current Establishment.

In order to challenge the government's theory of the facts, Weinglass and Kunstler urged the jury not to believe the government witnesses, especially those who were undercover police officers who had infiltrated the Yippies' meetings for organizing the protests.

The defense attorneys called witnesses who would testify that the real intent of the defendants was to demonstrate peacefully and hold the Festival of Life. James Hunt testified that he saw marshals trying to push a crowd of protesters away from a group of police officers. According to Hunt, the helmeted officers marched straight into the crowd for a hundred yards, beating people all the way. "The attack was simply a punitive assault upon the crowd. There was no provocation."[5]

The defense also called Sarah Diamant to the stand. At the time of the riots in Chicago, Diamant was a teacher at Cornell University, while working on a degree. As part of a project, Sarah Diamant filmed some of the many conflicts between police and demonstrators during the convention week riots. She testified that although she had nothing in her hands other than a camera and microphone and never assaulted a police officer, she was beaten and gassed by the police.

Sarah Diamant described to the jury how it felt being gassed with Mace, a nerve gas used by some police departments to disable an attacker:

> My eyes and the skin all around the top of my face were burning. I put my hand up because it hurt, and sort of clawed

at it, and . . . the moment I put my hand on the skin and pulled it down, the burning followed my hand right down my face, and I wanted to throw up, and I couldn't. I just kept gagging.[6]

Weinglass attempted to show that whatever violence occurred during convention week was caused by police aggression and unnecessary force. For that purpose, the defense called Ruth Migdal to the stand. Migdal had

Demonstrators at the Hilton Hotel in Chicago duck as a police officer squirts Mace, a painful, disabling chemical, into the crowd.

provided first aid at two major confrontations between demonstrators and police.

Ruth Migdal testified that on August 25, 1968, she followed a line of police officers that was trying to clear the park after curfew had been announced. Although the park was peaceful at that point, the situation quickly became violent as the officers got close to the crowd. One officer in charge was saying, "Hold it. Hold it." Migdal said, "He was losing control. They were pushing past him, and they started beating people on the heads."[7]

Migdal also testified that on August 28, 1968, she saw

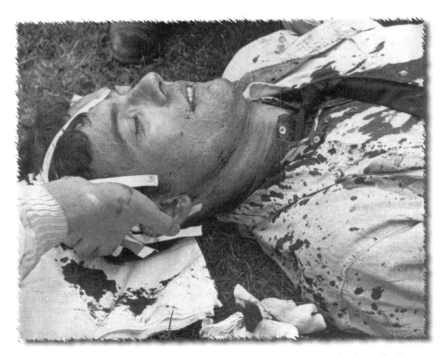

Many demonstrators were injured in the protests that took place during the convention. This unidentified man is receiving first aid.

"red-faced, blue-helmeted, blue-shirted . . . [policemen], their arms up, a club in one arm, coming out of [a] bus at full speed chanting, 'Kill, kill, kill,' and then go across the street and charge into the crowd and start beating heads."[8]

Kunstler and Weinglass also reminded the court that the defendants had made an effort to get permits to hold their marches and demonstrations, but that they were denied. According to the defense, the city of Chicago decided to prevent the large demonstrations during convention week because they wanted to avoid embarrassment to the city as host of the Democratic National Convention.

The defense claimed that the decision not to allow permits for a demonstration was unconstitutional. The city's denial of the defendants' constitutional right to free speech was an act of provocation, which made a confrontation between demonstrators and police inevitable.

Celebrities Testify

A number of witnesses to the riots in Lincoln Park testified about what they remembered about the events that actually took place in the summer of 1968. However, in order for the defendants to be found guilty, the jury had to believe that they had intended to cause violence in Chicago while they were making their plans for the Festival of Life, and even before that, when they traveled to Chicago from out of state.

In order to show that the Chicago Seven had intended to have a peaceful demonstration, attorneys Kunstler and Weinglass called several witnesses who had been involved in the early planning stages of the demonstrations. These witnesses included a number of well-known artists, singers, actors, and poets. While these celebrities gave testimony about the witnesses' intentions, they also baffled the judge and observers with their behavior in the courtroom.

One witness, Ed Sanders, described his occupation as poet, songwriter, leader of a rock and roll band, publisher, editor, recording artist, "peace-creep," and yodeler. Allen Ginsberg, who was a famous poet and writer during the 1960s, also testified on behalf of the defense. Ginsberg related conversations he had with the defendant Abbie Hoffman during the planning stages of the Festival of Life. However, his testimony also included chanting in Sanskrit, the ancient poetic language of India.

Allen Ginsberg's lengthy explanations about the need for chanting, threats to the ecology, and eastern philosophy left the judge in laughter. The prosecution grew increasingly impatient, and the defense attorneys became indignant because the witness was apparently not taken seriously by the court.

Another artist who took the stand on behalf of the defendants was singer Judy Collins. Collins attempted to perform her hit song "Where Have All the Flowers Gone?" as part of her testimony. Judge Hoffman immediately put a stop to the performance. However, she did support the defense's theory that the Chicago Seven had attempted to get permits from the city officials.

Collins said that "if the City of Chicago wanted to provoke violence and wanted to provoke unrest, all they had to do was continue ignoring our requests for grants and also continue the kind of things that had been happening."[9] Judy Collins also testified that she eventually decided not to perform at the Festival of Life because she was frightened by police brutality she had seen on television.[10]

Norman Mailer was a prominent writer who had been asked to speak at the Festival of Life. Mailer told the court about Jerry Rubin's plans for the demonstrations during convention week. Rather than showing any intent to cause violence, Mr. Mailer claimed that Rubin's plans would only highlight the Establishment's readiness for violence.

According to Norman Mailer, Rubin expected that the presence of thousands of young people at the festival would terrify the Establishment so badly that Lyndon B. Johnson would have to be nominated under guard. He said Rubin also claimed that the protesters would just "be there and they won't be able to take it."[11] According to Mailer, Rubin had said that the Establishment would "smash the city themselves. [The Establishment] will provoke all the violence."[12]

At the same time, Mailer related the determination of the Chicago Seven to hold their demonstrations whether or not the city granted permits. Mailer testified that David Dellinger never wanted to do anything that would cause violence. However, Dellinger claimed that if they avoided everything that could possibly result in violence, they would never be able to protest anything at all.

Two further witnesses gave evidence that any violence that occurred had been caused by excessive use of force by police. According to these famous witnesses, they had come to expect unprovoked violent attacks from police departments throughout the country. Singer and actor Arlo Guthrie told Abbie Hoffman that it would be difficult for him to "get involved in that kind of thing because we had had a lot of trouble before with festivals and gatherings because of police violence."[13]

Jesse Jackson, a minister and emerging leader in the African-American community, told the jury about his meeting with Rennie Davis. Although he wanted to participate in the demonstrations, Jackson confessed that he had "heard rumblings" that if African Americans participated in a big demonstration, they would be "shot down" by police.[14]

Jackson told Davis that he was "afraid of the tremendous police build up in [his] community, so we felt too helpless to just put our heads in a meat grinder," and for that reason, he would spend his time "working in the black community telling blacks not to get involved."[15]

Testimony From the Chicago Seven

On December 23, 1969, those following the trial of the Chicago Seven were finally able to hear the defendants testify on their own behalf. If the celebrity witnesses brought a bizarre atmosphere to the courtroom, the testimony of the seven defendants only increased that impression.

For the most part, each of the seven defendants denied that they had planned any sort of violence in Chicago during convention week and that they never encouraged anyone else to perform violent acts.

The first of the Chicago Seven to take the witness stand

was Abbie Hoffman. Hoffman rejected society in its present form by the way he lived his life and the way he approached the world. Even his manner of identifying himself in the courtroom showed his distaste for the trappings of life in the United States.

Abbie Hoffman described himself as an "orphan of America." When asked for his date of birth, Abbie Hoffman answered that he was "psychologically" born in 1966. He described his residence as "Woodstock Nation," which was a "state of mind . . . dedicated to cooperation versus competition."[16]

Judge Hoffman grew impatient with the defendant who shared his last name. Judge Hoffman insisted that Abbie Hoffman give his place of residence. The judge directed the witness: "Nothing about philosophy or India, sir. Just where you live if you have a place to live."[17]

Although Abbie Hoffman insisted that he and the other demonstrators never intended to cause violence, the prosecution tried to bring out the fact that the city of Chicago had good reason to deny permits to an irresponsible group. Schultz asked whether or not it was true that the Yippies were trying to create a situation where the government would have to bring in the army and National Guard. The prosecution's theory was that Hoffman and his followers desired this action on the part of the city so that it would appear that the convention had to be held under military conditions.

Hoffman replied, "You can do that with a yo-yo in this

Abbie Hoffman laughs during a conversation with a reporter in New York City on September 16, 1969.

country. . . . You can see just from this courtroom. Look at all the troops around."[18]

The Summation

After almost five months of testimony and nearly constant outbursts in the courtroom, the trial of the Chicago Seven was almost at an end. However, both the prosecution and the defense had one final opportunity to address the jury. During closing arguments, each side has the chance to sum up their most convincing arguments and remind the jury of those facts that most strongly support their position. William Kunstler addressed the jury first for the defense.

Kunstler began by wondering aloud whether the Chicago Seven had received a fair trial. He continued by reminding the court that the seven defendants had a right under the United States Constitution to travel, to dissent, and to agitate for dissent.

Kunstler compared the activities of his clients to those of the Boston Tea Party demonstrators in 1773. American colonists wished to show their anger at having to pay a British tax when they bought tea, which was a popular beverage before America's Revolutionary War. As colonists, Americans were not truly represented in Parliament, England's lawmaking body. Colonists claimed that it was unjust for England to impose taxes without waiting to hear any arguments against yet another tax. "No taxation without representation" became the rallying cry in colonial America.

In order to demonstrate their opposition to the tax on tea, some colonists disguised themselves as American Indians, crept to the Custom House (where the import tax on tea was collected) and threw all available crates of tea into Boston Harbor. Here, the defense attorney made his most powerful argument. The protesters in 1968 were denied the right to demonstrate in front of the amphitheater, where the main events of the Democratic Convention were to take place.

Kunstler acknowledged that David Stahl would have given a permit for demonstrations away from the amphitheater. However, Kunstler said, that would have been like telling Boston patriots to "go anywhere you want, but don't go to the Custom House, because . . . it was at the Custom House and it was at the Amphitheater that the protesters wanted to show that something was terribly and totally wrong."[19]

Just as it was symbolic for the Boston patriots to protest the new tea tax at the place where it would be collected, the need to protest at the amphitheater was symbolic to the Chicago protesters.

As to the claim that Lee Weiner had attempted to fire-bomb the underground parking garage, Kunstler answered simply that it never happened. "There never was any such plot and you can prove it to yourselves. Nothing was ever found, and there is no visible proof of this at all. No bottles. No rags . . . No gasoline."[20]

The defense attorney concluded by reminding the jury of the many social conflicts that were raging at that time in the United States. The war, racism, and poverty were "terrible problems . . . so enormous that they stagger the imagination. But they don't go away by destroying their critics."[21]

According to Kunstler, the only solution was for people like the defendants to continually speak out against everything they felt was wrong.

Prosecution's Closing Arguments

Thomas Foran made the closing arguments on behalf of the government. The prosecutor suggested to the jury that the Chicago Seven had a very strange way of arguing that they planned no violence in Chicago. Foran summed up the defense's attitude toward the several undercover police officers who testified against the defendants.

According to Foran, the defense claimed that because the officers were undercover agents for the police, they could not be honest men. Foran called that argument "a gross statement" and reminded the jury that some of the bravest men in law enforcement made their contributions while undercover.

Foran also reminded the jury that the seven defendants were not the "young kids" the defense pretended them to be. Although Kunstler called them by childlike names—Rennie, Abbie, and Jerry—the jury had to remember that the Chicago Seven were sophisticated, highly educated men. And David Dellinger was far from a "young kid" at fifty-two. Foran then went so far as to say that the Chicago Seven were "evil men."[22] This statement drew laughter from several courtroom observers.

Next, the prosecutor reminded the jury of his theory that the Chicago Seven intended to provoke the police into violence. Foran said that a police officer who was faced with a protester who was resisting arrest and screaming "police brutality" had to make a choice. The police officer can either "physically subdue" the protester there on the spot or call for help.

In some cases, the officer might "get tough" and "crack" the protester. While Foran acknowledged that this is wrong, he also noted that in Chicago, the crowd had taken this as justification to attack the police with rocks and bottles and claim that they were merely defending themselves. According to Foran, the technique was simple. The jurors had seen the same tactics used during the trial, he said.

Finally, Foran told the jury that the Chicago Seven took advantage of the young people who saw all that was wrong in the United States. After the assassinations of John and Bobby Kennedy and Martin Luther King, Jr., Americans were disillusioned. The seven defendants took advantage of that feeling of helplessness and used it to corrupt "those kids" for their own intentions. Those intentions, Thomas Foran stated, were to "disrupt . . . To force the use of troops . . . to intimidate the establishment so much it will smash the city."[23]

With Foran's closing argument, the presentation of the trial of the Chicago Seven came to a finish. The prosecutors and the defense attorneys had done everything they could. The question of whether or not the Chicago Seven were guilty of violating the 1968 Anti-Riot Act would have to be answered by a jury of ten women and two men.

chapter seven

THE DECISION

THE JURY—The Chicago Seven defendants had received a trial before twelve jurors, who would now decide the issue of whether they were innocent or guilty of the charges against them.

On February 14, 1970, the case of the Chicago Seven was given to the jury. The twelve jurors selected by the prosecutors and defense attorneys were then allowed to discuss the case. Until that point, they had been cautioned by the judge not to discuss or form an opinion about the evidence they had seen and heard.

Now, the jury had to go over the evidence, discuss the arguments from both sides of the case, and decide whether the defendants were guilty or not guilty. If found not guilty, the defendants would be allowed to go free. If found guilty, the defendants faced the possibility of a jail sentence and a fine.

Contempt of Court

Before the jury could finish deliberating on the charges against the defendants,

Judge Hoffman kept a promise he had made to the defendants and their attorneys many times during the course of the trial. With the jury deliberating on the criminal charges, Hoffman addressed the problem of the many contempt of court violations against the Chicago Seven and their lawyers.

Judge Julius Hoffman listed more than 150 instances of contempt of court, remarking that the "offenders have engaged in such impudent repetition of their misconduct" that he felt it was fair to impose consecutive sentences.[1] After finding the seven defendants and the two defense attorneys guilty of each and every count of contempt of court, the judge proceeded to distribute sentences for the acts of contempt.

Among the many events listed was the episode in which defendant Abbie Hoffman blew a kiss to the jury. Abbie Hoffman was sentenced to one day in prison for that act. However, other violations, such as refusal to rise when the judge entered or left the room, brought lengthier sentences.

Judge Hoffman also found attorney William Kunstler guilty of contempt for telling Judge Hoffman that there was "no law in this court." By the time Judge Hoffman finished dealing with the contempt charges, the defendants and their attorney had been sentenced to staggering sentences for their acts of contempt alone. This is especially remarkable, since the jury had not yet reached a verdict on the main charges against the defendants. The Chicago Seven would have to serve time in jail for the contempt of court charges

Awaiting the verdict, three of the Chicago Seven defendants take questions from the press. From left are Abbie Hoffman, Rennie Davis, and Jerry Rubin.

even if they were found innocent on the original conspiracy charges.

When the judge finished reciting the contempt sentences, the results were immense. David Dellinger, Rennie Davis, and Jerry Rubin were each sentenced to more than two years in jail. Tom Hayden, Abbie Hoffman, and attorney Leonard Weinglass each received sentences of approximately one year. Tom Froines was sentenced to six months in jail. Lee Weiner received least of all, with a sentence of little more than two months.

The judge handed attorney William Kunstler the

heaviest sentence of all—four years and thirteen days in jail. According to the judge, Kunstler had asked one witness no fewer than eighty-three questions that were "objectionable . . . and suggestive."[2]

As the sentences were being announced, the defendants reacted with outbursts that had become almost commonplace. Rennie Davis interrupted to tell the judge that he represented "all that is old, ugly, bigoted, and repressive in this country, and I will tell you that the spirit at this defense table is going to devour your sickness in the next generation."[3]

Attorney William Kunstler reacted to the four-year sentence by telling the judge that he had "tried with all of [his] heart faithfully to represent [his] clients" in the face of what he considered "repressive and unjust conduct toward them." He finished: "If I have to pay with my liberty for such repression, then that is the price of my beliefs. . . ."[4]

What Judge Hoffman did was to act as prosecutor, judge, and jury in the matter of the contempt charges. Hoffman did not allow any arguments on the defendants' point of view. He did not allow an uninvolved party to decide whether they should be tried at all for contempt.

Further, the judge avoided the legal requirement that any sentence of more than six months required a trial by jury. He accomplished this by addressing each instance of contempt, finding the defendant or attorney guilty, and assigning individual sentences for up to six months for each crime.

Many attorneys and courtroom observers denounced this manner of sentencing for contempt.[5] The late Supreme

Court justice Felix Frankfurter had written that precisely because judges are human, judges would take contempt of court personally. For that reason alone, the judge should not judge those who offended him, unless it becomes necessary in order for the trial to proceed.

The Jury

While Judge Hoffman was reading the sentences imposed for the contempt violations, the jury was taken to the jury room, where they were to deliberate over the conspiracy charges against the Chicago Seven.

The jury had been presented with two very different views of the events surrounding the Chicago convention. The government had presented evidence to indicate that the demonstrators had charged the police, "throwing bags full of urine and spiked balls."[6] For its part, the defense had presented evidence to show that the police had charged the demonstrators, wildly swinging their clubs.

However, the jury had to make only three decisions in the end. They had to decide whether John Froines and Lee Weiner were guilty of teaching how to build and use a fire-bomb. Next, the jury was required to decide whether there was, in fact, a conspiracy, or agreement, among all seven defendants to work together to cause a riot.

The final charge against all seven defendants was crossing state lines with the intent to incite a riot and then performing some acts in order to cause that riot. The acts specified by the prosecution were the many speeches given by the defendants during convention week.

As the jury began to consider the charges against the defendants, they found that eight jurors believed all the defendants were guilty of both conspiracy and of crossing state lines with the intent to cause a riot. The remaining jurors felt that all defendants were innocent of both charges.[7] During the course of almost four days of deliberating, none of the jurors changed his or her mind.

In the American legal system, a jury must deliberate, or discuss the evidence, until they come to a unanimous decision. While they may attempt to persuade the "holdout" jurors, they cannot compromise, or bargain among themselves, to reach a decision upon which all agree. However, it would later be reported that that is exactly how the jury for the Chicago Seven reached a verdict.

Kay Richards later said that she acted as a mediator. Although several of the jurors cried out of frustration and anger, they were able to send a note to the judge stating that they had reached a unanimous verdict. One courtroom observer noted that it was the perfect conclusion—a political verdict for a political trial.[8]

The jury found both John Froines and Lee Weiner innocent on the charge of making a bomb. All seven defendants were acquitted, or found not guilty, on the conspiracy count. However, five of the men had been separately charged with crossing state lines with the intent to create a riot and giving speeches for that purpose. Abbie Hoffman, Jerry Rubin, David Dellinger, Rennie Davis, and Tom Hayden were all found guilty of that final charge.

On February 20, 1970, Judge Hoffman sentenced each

of the five men to five years in prison, a fine of $5,000, and the cost of holding the trial, which amounted to nearly $50,000.[9] If the defendants were dismayed by their sentences, none of them showed it in court. Jerry Rubin presented Judge Hoffman with a copy of his book, which he autographed for the judge. The book was inscribed with a message for the judge: "Julius, You radicalized more young people than we ever could. You're the country's top Yippie."[10]

Tom Hayden asked the judge why the government made martyrs of the defendants. "If you had given us a permit, very little would have happened in Chicago."[11] Rennie Davis promised Foran that he would move next door to the prosecutor's family. Davis claimed that as the boy next door, he would "turn the sons and daughters of the ruling class into Viet Cong."[12] Davis was referring to the Vietnamese communist fighters who were a constant danger to American soldiers in Vietnam. In effect, Davis was promising to turn the children of America's lawmakers against their own parents.

David Dellinger said he only wished that the Chicago Seven and other radicals were "smarter, more dedicated, more united."[13] If they were better at communicating, Dellinger claimed, then people like the prosecutors and Judge Hoffman would have been convinced of the need of "the revolution."[14]

Other than complaining about the conditions in the county jail, Abbie Hoffman said little. However, he did remind the judge that Thomas Jefferson had called for a revolution every ten years.[15]

The trial had come to a disappointing end for five of the Chicago Seven, as they had been sentenced to heavy fines and time in jail. On another note, however, some of the defendants felt that they had scored a victory—they had captured the attention of the media and many Americans.

Abbie Hoffman had warned the city of Chicago long before the convention began that "the world is watching." The world had, in fact, been watching, and many observers were convinced that the Establishment was a corrupt machine in serious need of repairs. Even *The New York Times* carried an editorial stating that the charges against the Chicago Seven were questionable. The editor wrote further that the trial opened the way for the radicals to use the courtroom for their propaganda.[16] Judge Hoffman merely helped the defendants in their campaign with his biased behavior.

Still, the matter of the Chicago Seven was far from over. American defendants found guilty of a crime have the right to appeal the decision of the trial court. Although they are only permitted to have one trial before a jury to consider the facts of the case, legal mistakes in the courtroom can be the basis of another trial. William Kunstler immediately began such an appeal on behalf of the five convicted members of the Chicago Seven.

chapter eight

THE APPEAL

BAIL REQUEST—When a convicted criminal does not present a threat to the public, the attorneys for the defendant ask the judge to set bail. This means that a certain amount of money is deposited with the court and the convicted person need not go directly to prison. Instead, the money acts as security that the defendant will show up in court as required by the judge while the attorneys pursue an appeal. The defendant, meanwhile, does not have to go to jail.

When the five members of the Chicago Seven were convicted, their attorneys immediately asked Judge Hoffman to set bail. At the same time, attorneys Kunstler and Weinglass asked the judge to set bail for their clients and themselves for the sentences received for the contempt of court violations.

Judge Hoffman refused to set bail on any of the charges, so both attorneys and their clients were sent directly to jail. Within hours, William Kunstler and

Leonard Weinglass had another lawyer appeal Hoffman's decision to refuse bail. The defense attorneys were released that same day, and their clients followed them to relative freedom in less than two weeks.[1]

Simply because the men were free on bail did not mean that they were free of the convictions. Lawyers and clients alike would have to serve the sentences imposed for contempt if the appellate court affirmed the trial court's decision. David Dellinger, Abbie Hoffman, Jerry Rubin, Rennie Davis, and Tom Hayden would also have to pay a fine and serve time in prison for their convictions under the 1968 Anti-Riot Act.

Therefore, two separate appeals were made to the United States Court of Appeals for the Seventh Circuit. One appeal addressed the contempt charges; the second was directed at the five defendants' convictions under the Anti-Riot Act.

On February 8, 1972, the appellate court heard arguments on the Chicago Seven's conviction for traveling among the states with the intent to cause a riot and performing some acts toward causing such riots to occur.

The three-judge panel first concluded that the Anti-Riot Act was constitutional. That is, they rejected the argument that the statute, or law, violated the defendants' right to freedom of expression under the First Amendment to the United States Constitution. The court did agree with the defendants that actions made for the sole purpose of expressing views on a political topic are well within the area of protected speech.[2]

However, the court added that simply because certain

actions, such as demonstrations and protest marches, are meant as a form of speech, that did not automatically mean that the government could not pass a law putting some limits on that form of speech. Moreover, it was up to the government to show that the defendants' actions were more "action" than "speech" and therefore removed from First Amendment protection.

Judge Thomas E. Fairchild, writing the Court of Appeals decision, noted that in order for a political action to lose the constitutional protection given to speech, that action "must have a very substantial capacity to propel action. . . . The real question is whether particular speech is intended to and has such capacity to propel action that it is reasonable to treat such speech as action."[3]

According to the appellate judges, the Anti-Riot Act adequately described the sort of "disorder" that must be treated as action, rather than speech. Actions did not receive the same First Amendment protection as speech. Therefore, the Chicago Seven's challenge to the constitutionality of the Anti-Riot Act failed.

Selection of the Jury

The Court of Appeals next addressed the manner in which the jury had been selected for the trial of the Chicago Seven. During jury selection, both the defense attorneys and the prosecutors are allowed to ask questions of the men and women being considered to serve on the jury.

Both defense and prosecution have a certain number of chances to decide that a particular juror will not be allowed to sit on the jury. These "peremptory" challenges are made without having to state a reason for excusing a prospective juror from serving. The attorneys may also excuse an unlimited number of prospective jurors if they can show a valid reason why that candidate for jury service should not serve. Such reasons might include the juror's own admission that he or she cannot be impartial or knows one of the parties to the lawsuit.

During jury selection for the trial of the Chicago Seven, the defense attorneys wanted Judge Hoffman to ask prospective jurors whether they had any friends or relatives who were in law enforcement. Obviously, Kunstler and Weinglass wanted this question answered in order to discover any prejudice favoring police officers.

Although Judge Hoffman did ask this question of the first twelve prospective jurors, he did not make an effort to ask this of any of the remaining men and women being considered for jury service. Hoffman told the defense attorneys that he had reached the conclusion that questioning potential jurors about their possible relationship with law enforcement officers and other inquiries into their opinions on current matters were not relevant to the trial.

The appellate court did not believe that a prospective juror is always aware of his own prejudice. Therefore, according to the court, the defense attorneys should have been granted their request to ask questions about the jurors' backgrounds and attitudes in order to make informed decisions about a juror's fitness for service.

Since the case involved current matters such as the

United States' involvement in the Vietnam War, it was reasonable to think that the jurors would have some opinion about the case. The appellate judges did not believe that Judge Hoffman could "safely assume, without inquiry, that the [jurors] had no serious prejudice on this subject, or could recognize such prejudices and lay them aside."[4]

Although the panel of appellate judges mentioned that some of the questions submitted by the defense attorneys were "inappropriate," they noted that other questions would have shown a juror's attitude toward long hair, different lifestyles, and protests in general. The court held that defense had a right to ask those questions in an attempt to prevent unfairness at trial. For these reasons, the appellate court found that Judge Hoffman's refusal to ask these questions was an error.

The Jury's Communication with Judge and Marshal

Months after the verdict had been given, the defendants read a magazine article that claimed that Judge Hoffman and the courtroom marshal had had some communications with the jury and that those messages had not been mentioned to either defense or prosecution attorneys at the time of the trial.

Such communications are considered to be a serious error during a trial. A trial attorney should be made aware of every such communication in order to guard against having any outside party influence the jury, either by accident or on purpose.

The appellate court asked that the matter be investigated. Based on that investigation, the appellate court found that the jury had sent at least one note to Judge Hoffman, stating that they were unable to reach a verdict. Another instance involved a court marshal telling the jurors that the "judge can keep you here as long as he wants."[5]

The defense attorneys claimed, and the appellate court agreed, that the defense attorneys should have been made aware that the jury had sent a message to the judge claiming that they could not agree on a verdict. Since the defense suspected that the jury might have decided on a verdict through compromise, these messages could have given the judge a chance to remind jurors of their responsibility to reach a verdict through persuasion.

The appellate court also decided that the remarks made to the sequestered jury by the marshal might have influenced the jury to arrive at a verdict by any means possible. The court noted that it was impossible to tell if any harm had been done by these communications. Since the court could not say with certainty that the communications were harmless, the judges decided that issue alone was grounds for reversal of the conspiracy.

The Judge's Behavior

Attorneys for the defense also complained that the attitude of the judge toward the Chicago Seven and their attorneys during the trial must have influenced the jurors' judgment. The appellate court noted that the defendants' behavior in the courtroom required correction from the judge. However, the panel of judges went on to state that there was a high standard for the behavior of judges, and improper actions by defendants and their attorneys does not give the judge any reason to behave with less dignity.

Judge Fairchild remarked that Judge Hoffman had made several statements in the presence of the jury that were sarcastic, "implying that defense counsel was inept . . . or untrustworthy." Judge Hoffman's comments revealed his "antagonistic attitude toward the defense."[6] Judge Fairchild also noted that many of the comments made by the prosecutor went beyond the boundaries of making proper characterizations of the defendants.

According to the appellate court judges, the behavior of the trial judge and prosecutors in the courtroom was improper and would have required reversal even if the other errors had not occurred. Therefore, on November 21, 1972, the appellate court ordered the judgments against the five defendants reversed. The effect of the reversal was that the convictions were erased, and the case was sent back to the trial court for a retrial, if the prosecutors wished to try the matter again.

Appealing the Contempt of Court Decisions

On May 11, 1972, the United States Court of Appeals for the Seventh Circuit announced its decision on the appeal that both attorneys and seven defendants made of Judge Hoffman's sentences for their contempt of court violations.

Judge Walter J. Cummings wrote the decision for the three-judge panel. The judge noted that both Weinglass and Kunstler had subjected Judge Hoffman to many insults and verbal attacks. In fact, the attorneys' conduct was so offensive, it tended to produce actual prejudice toward them on the part of the trial judge.

Judge Cummings also wrote that the defendants in the conspiracy trial had antagonized Judge Hoffman. He noted, "The trial judge himself felt that all the defendants worked [together] at baiting the judge."[7] Since the acts of contempt were personally directed at Judge Hoffman, the judge could hardly be considered unbiased.

Furthermore, the three-judge panel decided that Hoffman's treatment of each charge of contempt separately deprived the defendants of their right to a trial by jury when the penalty would be more than a six-month jail sentence. For these reasons, the appellate court ordered that the contempt of court charges be presented before another judge.

William Kunstler made a prediction that the government would not hold another trial for the Chicago Seven. He was proven partially correct in January 1973, when the government announced that the defendants would not be retried on the original charges but would be retried on contempt charges.

In December 1973, Judge Edward Gignoux heard the evidence against the Chicago Seven and their attorneys. All but thirteen charges of alleged contempt were dropped. However, Judge Gignoux imposed no fine or sentence for the charges that remained. More than five years after the convention week, the legal process involving the Chicago Seven had come to a close. Still, the movement sparked by the Chicago demonstrations was far from complete.

chapter nine

AFTER THE DECISION

AFTERMATH—While the trial of the Chicago Seven had finally come to a close, not all the matters surrounding convention week were resolved at that trial. The eight Chicago police officers who were charged with interfering with the civil rights of the demonstrators had all been found not guilty. However, one of the officers had lost his job; the others had been suspended for a brief period of time.[1]

Bobby Seale, whose case had been dealt with apart from the other seven defendants in the Chicago conspiracy trial, could not be retried for the conspiracy charges against him. The other seven defendants had been found not guilty of the conspiracy charges. Therefore, there was no one left for Seale to have conspired, or planned with, to commit a crime.

Students and others carried on the task of protest started by the Chicago Seven. However, the police brutality that many Americans criticized during convention week in Chicago would soon pale in comparison to measures taken in 1970.

One thousand college students rallied at Kent State University in Ohio on May 4, 1970, to protest the United States invasion of Cambodia. Demonstrators took to the streets for two days, and windows were broken. After an old ROTC building was burned, the Akron mayor called the National Guard. Guardsmen opened fire, and four young people were killed. Eight others were wounded.[2] This horrible event brought mixed reactions from Americans. One historian wrote that the killings were the Establishment's way of telling protesters that the "politics of confrontation had become a life-threatening activity."[3]

New York City construction workers took the opposite view. On May 8, 1970, the "hard hats" broke up an antiwar demonstration and forced City Hall to raise the American flag to full staff position. The flag had been lowered to half-staff to recognize the four young people killed at Kent State. The construction workers apparently felt that such an honor should be reserved for American soldiers who had served their country, and not those who opposed the country's involvement in Vietnam. Richard Nixon, who was president of the United States at the time, stated that college war protesters were "bums."[4]

The Winds of Change

The trial of the Chicago Seven brought the winds of change from the streets into the courtroom. Rather than simply turning to an alternative lifestyle, young Americans sought to bring about change in the social structure through legal means. While the Chicago riots came about mostly as a protest of the Vietnam War and racism in the United States, other issues requiring change in the United States also entered the legal system.

While the attorneys for the Chicago Seven were working on their appeal, another man tested the boundaries of free speech. Daniel Ellsberg was a former employee of the United States Department of Defense. He stole a forty-seven-volume study, "US Decision-Making Process on Vietnam Policy." The study, known as the "Pentagon Papers," was labeled "Top Secret" by the government.

Ellsberg passed the report to *The New York Times* and *The Washington Post*. Both newspapers began running a series of portions taken from the stolen report. The government tried to enjoin, or prevent, the newspapers from printing the top-secret reports. Like the trial of the Chicago Seven, the Pentagon Papers case inspired heated debate about whether national security was more important than freedom of expression. On June 30, 1971, the United States Supreme Court rendered its decision in the matter.

Justice Hugo Black, writing for the Court, rejected the government's argument that the newspapers must be restrained from printing the documents on the basis of national security. It was the conclusion of the Supreme Court that the "history and language of the First Amendment support the view that the press must be left free to publish news, whatever the source, without censorship, injunctions, or prior restraints."[5]

Once numbers of an underground movement, protesters had gained acceptance in many areas of American life. The legal system in the United States was beginning to allow greater freedom of speech and forms of expression. Abbie Hoffman's warning that "the world was watching" had been proven correct, and as the world watched, they saw that the Chicago Seven trial was only the beginning of the movement.

chapter ten

THE CHICAGO SEVEN TODAY

UPDATE—When the trial in Chicago came to a close, many of the defendants and their attorneys found that the experience "branded them for life."[1] The group met annually, but over the years, their numbers dwindled. Jerry Rubin, founder of the Yippies, later organized a satirical theater version of the trial. The Yippie turned "yuppie" (Young Urban Professional) in the 1980s when he cut his hair, shaved his beard, and went to work on Wall Street. In 1985, he and Abbie Hoffman went on a tour debating the question, "Are you a Yippie or a yuppie?" Rubin died in 1994 when he was struck by a car while crossing the street.

Abbie Hoffman continued to organize protests, including demonstrations on issues relating to the environment. However, in 1973, Hoffman was arrested for the sale of cocaine, and he went into hiding for six years to avoid a life sentence. He suffered emotional breakdowns until his death by suicide in 1989.

William Kunstler went on to enjoy great fame and demand as an attorney. Over the years, he represented a number of controversial clients, such as Colin Ferguson, the Long Island Railroad mass murderer, and Jack Ruby, the killer of Lee Harvey Oswald. On September 4, 1995, William Kunstler died of heart failure. Before he died, however, Kunstler found forgiveness for Judge Julius Hoffman, who died in 1983. Kunstler called Judge Hoffman a "worthy opponent . . . (who) was only doing what the government told him to do."[2]

Thomas Foran, prosecutor during the trial of the Chicago Seven, turned to the private practice of law before his death in August 2000. Foran once remarked that the trial was "more than theater; it was vulgarity, threats, noise and foolishness."[3]

Those participants in the Chicago Seven trial who are alive have continued their efforts to improve those things they wish to change in the United States. Tom Hayden, who had struggled so hard against the established order, was eventually elected to be a state senator in California. When the 1996 Democratic National Convention was held once again in Chicago, Hayden was there as a delegate. He retired in 1999.

Rennie Davis, who had done most of the organization for the convention week demonstrations, later became a lecturer on such subjects as "Understanding Your Energy Signature," and "Unlocking Your Innocence."[4]

Lee Weiner also continued working for various causes.

Former Chicago Seven defendant Tom Hayden faced protesters and heckling as a California senator in 1997.

He has protested for Russian Jews, for the Anti-Defamation League, and for more funding for AIDS research.

David Dellinger also appeared in Chicago for the 1996 Democratic National Convention. At the time, he was eighty-one years old. Dellinger continues as an activist, having been arrested as recently as 1998 in Vermont. He was protesting the shipment of nuclear waste from Vermont to Texas.

John Froines, who had a background in chemistry at the time of the Chicago riots, went on to serve in Jimmy Carter's administration as presidential director of toxic

Bobby Seale (in front) and David Dellinger (behind Seale) lead a group onto the stage at a "60s Revisited" concert in Chicago, August 26, 1996.

substances. Later, he joined the faculty of University of California in Los Angeles, where he is director of the Center for Occupational and Environmental Health.

Bobby Seale now describes himself as an "old cripple-footed revolutionary humanist." Seale declined an offer to lead a group that would train young women and men to use weapons, claiming that he does not "live in the sixties." He has his own Web page, where he writes about such odd subjects as getting to the future by way of "DNA molecular revolutions."[5]

Those who worked so hard to change the world seem to have remained dedicated to that cause throughout their lives. The subject matter of their protests may have changed, but the Chicago Seven and Bobby Seale, along with their attorneys, remained dedicated to action and championing various causes. Similarly unchanged, the prosecutors and Judge Hoffman remained steadfastly conventional.

Although some of their methods may have been questionable, the Chicago Seven did capture the country's attention. Did their measures make people sit up and take notice while the uproar was at its peak only to lose the attention when the noise faded away? Or did the Chicago Seven make a lasting impression on mainstream America? Decide for yourself whether the trial of the Chicago Seven changed anything about the world in which the protesters lived.

Questions for Discussion

1. Consider the way in which the Chicago Seven delivered their message to mainstream America. Were their activities appropriate for persuading the Establishment to be more aware of differing viewpoints of existing problems? Or do you think that they simply wished to shock their audience? Explain your answer.

2. What other options were available to those who protested against the war in Vietnam? Talk to adults who were teenagers in 1968. Ask them whether they supported the United States' participation in the Vietnam War or were against it. If they protested the war, ask them what form that protest took.

3. Young people in 1968 often made their objections to the war known by using a symbol. Research the 1960s and early 1970s and find out about the various symbols that were used. Include the black armbands, MIA/POW wristbands, and the "peace" symbol. Discover the significance of each and the stories involved.

4. Look through a local newspaper to find an issue that is current in your neighborhood or city. This might be pollution, littering, or potholes in the city streets. Discuss with your classmates which issue is most urgent. Think of

ways that the problem could be brought to the attention of the authorities. Make sure your plan involves no harm to people or property, and follow through with your plan. Later, meet and discuss the results of your campaign to bring about change in your community.

5. Do you think that Chicago city officials made a mistake by not issuing permits for the Festival of Life? Why or why not?

6. What was the city hoping to avoid by not permitting the protesters to sleep in the parks and hold their marches? Did the city have any options?

Chapter Notes

Introduction

1. Todd Gitlin, *The Sixties: Years of Hope, Days of Rage* (New York: Bantam Books, 1987), p. 294.
2. Ibid., p. 5.
3. 18 USC ch. 102, Sec. 2101(a)(1), April 11, 1968.

Chapter 1. Two Faces of America

1. William Manchester, *The Glory and the Dream* (Boston: Little, Brown and Company, 1973), p. 1131.
2. J. Anthony Lukas, *The Barnyard Epithet and Other Obscenities* (New York: Harper & Row, 1970), p. 15.
3. Ibid., p. 20.
4. Ibid., p. 21.
5. David J. Langum, *William M. Kunstler: The Most Hated Lawyer in America* (New York: New York University Press, 1999), p. 104.
6. David Hilliard, "The Ideology of the Black Panther Party," *Douglass Archives of American Public Address*, June 7, 1999, <http://www.douglass.speech.nwu.edu/hill_a15.htm> (June 13, 2002).
7. Judith Clavir Albert and Stewart Edward Albert, *The Sixties Papers* (Westport, Conn.: Praeger Publishers, 1984), p. 32.
8. Ibid.
9. Abbie Hoffman, *The Autobiography of Abbie Hoffman* (New York: Four Walls Eight Windows, 1980), p. 144.
10. Lukas, p. 8.
11. Hoffman, p. 144.
12. Ibid.
13. Ibid., p. 154.
14. Ibid., pp. 146–147.
15. Albert and Albert, p. 32.

16. Ibid.

Chapter 2. The Convention

1. Daniel Walker, *Rights in Conflict: Chicago's Seven Brutal Days* (New York: Grosset & Dunlap, 1968).

2. Ibid.

3. Ibid., p. 82.

4. Ibid., p. 85.

5. Jeffrey St. John, *Countdown to Chaos* (Los Angeles: Nash Publishing, 1969), p. 65.

6. Jason Epstein, *The Great Conspiracy Trial* (New York: Random House, 1970), p. 310.

7. Walker, p. 91.

8. Douglas O. Linder, "The Chicago Seven Conspiracy Trial," *Famous Trials Page*, n.d., <www.law.umkc.edu/faculty/ projects/ftrials/Chicago7/Account.html> (August 25, 2000).

9. Abbie Hoffman, *The Autobiography of Abbie Hoffman* (New York: Four Walls Eight Windows, 1980), p. 156.

10. Linder.

11. Ibid.

12. "Episode 13: Make Love, Not War: The Sixties," *CNN Interactive Page*, n.d., <http://www.cnn.com/SPECIALS/cold.war/episodes/13/interviews/davis> (August 26, 2000).

13. Ibid.

14. Ibid.

15. Hoffman, pp. 159–160.

16. Linder.

17. Todd Gitlin, *The Sixties: Years of Hope, Days of Rage* (New York: Bantam Books, 1987), p. 332.

18. Jason Epstein, *The Great Conspiracy Trial* (New York: Random House, 1970), p. 79.

19. J. Anthony Lukas, *The Barnyard Epithet and Other Obscenities* (New York: Harper & Row, 1970), p. 2.

20. Linder.

21. *Time*, September 26, 1969, vol. 94, no. 13, p. 23.

Chapter 3. The Trial

1. *Time*, September 26, 1969, vol. 4, no. 13, p. 22.

2. Edward W. Knappman, ed., *Great American Trials* (Detroit: New England Publishing Associates, 1994), p. 589.

3. Judy Clavir and John Spitzer, editors, *The Conspiracy Trial* (Indianapolis, Ind.: The Bobbs-Merrill Company, 1970), p. 1.

4. David J. Langum, *William Kunstler: The Most Hated Lawyer in America* (New York University Press, 1999), p. 106.

5. Ibid., p. 107.

6. William Manchester, *The Glory and the Dream* (Boston: Little, Brown and Company, 1973) p. 207.

7. Ibid.

8. Langum, p. 108.

9. Ibid.

10. Epstein, p. 149.

11. Ibid.

12. Ibid., p. 153.

13. Ibid.

Chapter 4. The Prosecution's Case

1. *The Chicago Seven Trial: Famous Trials Page*, n.d., <http://www.law.umkc.edu/faculty/projects/ftrials/Chicago7/UsvDellinger.htm> (May 31, 2000).

2. Jason Epstein, *The Great Conspiracy Trial* (New York: Random House, 1970), p. 183.

3. Judy Clavir and John Spitzer, *The Conspiracy Trial* (Indianapolis, Ind.: The Bobbs-Merrill Company, 1970), p. 42.

4. Ibid.

5. Ibid.

6. "Testimony of Robert Murray, Prosecution Witness," *The Chicago Seven Trial: Famous Trials Page*, n.d., <http://www.law.umkc.edu/faculty/projects/ftrials/Chicago7/murray.html> (May 31, 2000).

7. Ibid.

8. Ibid.

9. Ibid.

10. Ibid.

11. Epstein, p. 183.

12. Ibid.

Chapter 5. Bobby Seale Objects

1 Jason Epstein, *The Great Conspiracy Trial* (New York: Random House, 1970), p. 231.

2. Jules Feiffer, *Pictures at a Prosecution* (New York: Grove Press, 1970), p. 29.

3. Judy Clavir and John Spitzer, *The Conspiracy Trial* (Indianapolis, Ind.: The Bobbs-Merrill Company, 1970), p. 153.

4. Ibid.

5. Feiffer, p. 30.

6. Ibid., p. 34.

7. Ibid.

8. Clavir and Spitzer, pp. 160–162.

9. Ibid., p. 162.

10. Ibid.

11. Ibid.

12. Feiffer, pp. 35–37.

13. David J. Langum, *William M. Kunstler: The Most Hated Lawyer in America* (New York University Press, 1999), p. 113.

14. Feiffer, pp. 37–38.

15. Abbie Hoffman, *The Autobiography of Abbie Hoffman* (New York: Four Walls Eight Windows, 1980), p. 196.

16. Feiffer, p. 45.

Chapter 6. The Defense

1. David J. Langum, *William M. Kunstler: The Most Hated Lawyer in America* (New York University Press, 1999), front cover.

2. Ibid.

3. Judy Clavir and John Spitzer, *The Conspiracy Trial* (Indianapolis, Ind.: The Bobbs-Merrill Company, 1970), p. 266.

4. Ibid., p. 267.

5. Ibid., p. 272.

6. "Testimony of Sarah Diamant," *The Chicago Seven Trial: Famous Trials Page*, n.d., <http://www.law.umkc.edu/faculty/projects/ftrials/Chicago7/diamant.html> (June 28, 2000).

7. Clavir and Spitzer, pp. 314–317.

8. Ibid., p. 315.

9. Ibid., p. 461.

10. Ibid., p. 462.

11. Ibid., pp. 492–493.

12. Ibid.

13. "Testimony of Arlo Guthrie," *The Chicago Seven Trial: Famous Trials Page*, n.d., <www.law.umkc.edu/faculty/projects/ftrials/Chicago7/Guthrie.html> (June 28, 2000).

14. "Testimony of Jesse Louis Jackson," *The Chicago Seven Trial: Famous Trials Page*, n.d., <http://www.law.umkc.edu/faculty/projects/ftrials/Chicago7/Jackson.html> (June 28, 2000).

15. Ibid.

16. Clavir and Spitzer, p. 344.

17. Ibid.

18. Jason Epstein, *The Great Conspiracy Trial* (New York: Random House, 1970), p. 352.

19. "Closing Arguments for the Defendants by Mr. Kunstler," *The Chicago Seven Trial: Famous Trials Page*, n.d., <http://www.law.umkc.edu/faculty/projects/ftrials/Chicago7/Closing.html> (June 11, 2000).

20. Ibid.

21. Ibid.

22. "Closing Arguments on Behalf of the Government by Mr. Foran," *The Chicago Seven Trial: Famous Trials Page*, n.d., <http://www.law.umkc.edu/faculty/projects/ftrials/Chicago7/Foranclose.html> (June 28, 2000).

23. Ibid.

Chapter 7. The Decision

1. Judy Clavir and John Spitzer, *The Conspiracy Trial* (Indianapolis, Ind.: The Bobbs-Merrill Company, 1970), p. 579.

2. Ibid., p. 614.

3. Ibid., p. 583.

4. David Langum, *William M. Kunstler: The Most Hated Lawyer in America* (New York University Press), p. 119.

5. J. Anthony Lukas, *The Barnyard Epithet and Other Obscenities* (New York: Harper & Row, 1970), p. 94.

6. Ibid., p. 95.

7. Ibid., p. 99.

8. Ibid., p. 101.

9. William Manchester, *The Glory and the Dream* (Boston: Little, Brown and Company, 1973), p. 1208.

10. Clavir and Spitzer, p. 599.

11. Jason Epstein, *The Great Conspiracy Trial* (New York: Random House, 1970), p. 428.

12. Ibid.

13. Epstein, p. 427.

14. Ibid.

15. Ibid., p. 429.

16. Langum, p. 120.

Chapter 8. The Appeal

1. David Langum, *William M. Kunstler: The Most Hated Lawyer in America* (New York University Press, 1999), p. 119.

2. "United States v. David Dellinger et al.," *The Chicago Seven Trial: Famous Trials Page*, n.d., <http://www.law.umkc.edu/faculty/projects/ftrials/Chicago7/USvDellinger.htm> (May 31, 2000).

3. Ibid.

4. Ibid.

5. Ibid.

6. Langum, p. 120.

7. "United States v. David Dellinger et al."

Chapter 9. After the Decision

1. Jason Epstein, *The Great Conspiracy Trial* (New York: Random House, 1970), pp. 432–433.

2. James Trager, *The People's Chronology* (New York: Henry Holt and Company, 1992), p. 1025.

3. Judith Clavir Albert and Stewart Edward Albert, *The Sixties Papers* (Westport, Conn.: Praeger Publishing, 1984), p. 54.

4. Trager.

5. Edward W. Knappman, ed., *Great American Trials* (Detroit: Visible Ink Press, 1994), p. 609.

Chapter 10. The Chicago Seven Today

1. David Langum, *William M. Kunstler: The Most Hated Lawyer in America* (New York: New York University Press, 1999), p. 121.

2. Ibid., p. 341.

3. "Chicago Seven Prosecutor Thomas A. Foran," obituary, *The Washington Post*, August 11, 2000, p. B7.

4. "Key Figures in the Chicago Seven Trial: Rennie Davis," *The Chicago Seven Trial: Famous Trials Page*, n.d., <www.law. umkc.edu/faculty/projects/ftrials/Chicago7/DavisR.htm> (April 10, 2001).

5. Bobby Seale, "Polylectic Reality," *Bobby Seale's R.E.A.C.H. Chronicles*, 1998, <http://www.bobbyseale.com/ polylectic.html> (June 13, 2002).

Glossary

appeal—A procedure in which a convicted person requests a higher court to review the decision of the trial court. An appeal will only address legal errors on the trial level. Factual issues decided by the jury cannot be challenged.

bail—An amount of money deposited with the court. This ensures that a defendant will return to court for trial.

conspire—An agreement between two or more people to commit a criminal act. Conspiracy is a crime in itself, separate from the planned crime, whether or not the crime is actually committed.

contempt—Words or actions showing disregard for the dignity of the court or disrupting the proceedings of the court. Contempt of court can be punished by jail time, fine, or both.

convention—A meeting of a political party's members, who are also elected representatives of individual states. Such meetings are held well in advance of presidential elections to nominate that party's candidate for the presidential election.

defendant—In criminal cases, a person who has been charged with committing a crime and has been brought to trial to determine his guilt or innocence.

Establishment—The existing power structure, whether government, legal, or corporate.

grand jury—A group of citizens who meet to determine whether enough evidence exists to charge a particular individual with a crime. This group does not determine guilt or innocence of a suspect.